Acknowledgements

Rosie Saddler, Bronanna Waterloo, Carolyn Tucker, Matt Killey, Maddie Dowling, Lee Burgemeestre, Ann James, Ann Haddon, Felicity Meakins, Josie Lardy.

Emma Aldus, Jayln Ahwon, Jesse Ahwon, Shontaria Ahwon, Tommy Barney, Timmy Birdum, Sharbina Birdum, Graham Chungulla, Joshua Gundari, Trivium Gundari, Kanelia Gundari, Emily Harrison, Jerome Laurie, Melanita Laurie, Michelle Laurie, Freddy Leering, Louiisianna Leering, Mason Leering, Matthew Leering, Lynettelie Leering, Kasey Leering, Tylas Lurda, Trevor Packsaddle, Josephena Roberts, Marcus Wallaby.

About the Indigenous Literacy Foundation

The Indigenous Literacy Foundation (ILF) is a national charity working with Aboriginal and Torres Strait Islander remote Communities across Australia. We are Community-led, responding to requests from remote Communities for culturally relevant books, including early learning board books, resources, and programs to support Communities to create and publish their stories in languages of their choice.

In 2024 the ILF won the Astrid Lindgren Memorial Award, given annually to a person or organisation for their outstanding contribution to children's or young adult literature.

First published in 2026 by the
Indigenous Literacy Foundation
Gadigal Country
Level 17/207 Kent Street
Sydney NSW 2000
ilf.org.au

Cataloguing-in-Publication details are available from the National Library of Australia

www.trove.nla.gov.au

ISBN 9781922592804

Typesetting and design by Lee Burgemeestre
Printed in China by RR Donnelley
Asia Printing Solutions Limited

Amanbidji Garu

Amanbidji Kids

by kids in the Amanbidji Community

INDIGENOUS LITERACY FOUNDATION™

Amanbidji,
Ngarinyman Country.
This is where we play.
This is our home.

We are
the garu
in Amanbidji.

Come with us and see
our favourite places.

Gedim my line,
gwigbala one!
Wiii!!!
Ei, Bronanna!
Catfish and turtle.
Luk darrei.

Bamboo Springs

Biggest mob in the troopy. We are off to Bamboo Springs. It's our favourite place to swim. We jump off the rope and take a bogi, but we have to collect the wood for the fire first. Rosie makes sure we help.

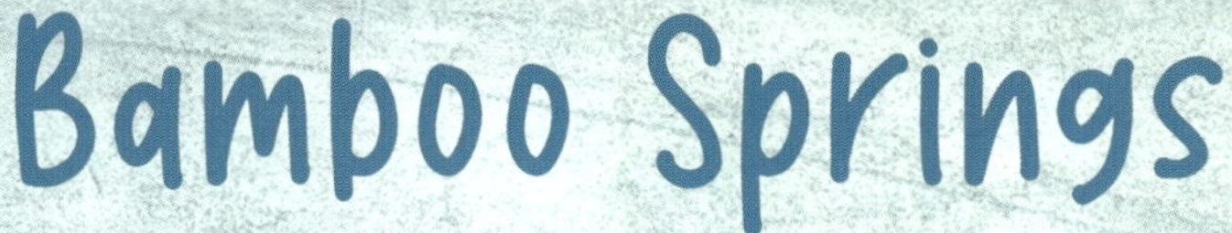

Bamboo Springs

One time we went driving to Bamboo Springs.
We nearly got there but ... the troopy got bogged.
Miss Carolyn was worried but we thought it was funny.

We went back to the first creek and made fire
to cook the kangaroo tail.

Hahaha
He rait,
wi wok
brom iya!

The Dam

When we come to the dam,
we sometimes see jabiru here.
Then we get mussels to eat.

Luk darrei. Jabiru!

The Dam

One time we went to the dam to get mussels and Mr Matt brought his boat.

Come on, we'll show you how to catch mussels with your feet. Then let's go bogi!
Marcus ran around the dam five times to try catch the boat.

I got a lot in my shirt.

Muddy feet.
We love you, Mr Matt.
I can feel it, a big fat one here!
Got one, got one! Biggest mob of mussels.

Nganjani

Our river, Nganjani, is long way from camp – 20 kilometres.

Sometimes we walk there, even in the hot time.
It gets hot, maybe 45 degrees.

We do lots of fishing, cooking and eating. We get dan.yan, and then we catch the barra, bream, catfish and other yawu. Sometimes we even catch croc. We cook them on the fire. If we see girrawa, we catch 'em and cook 'em on the fire too.

Im hotwanbala!!!
Gu bogi!
Lukad!
We have to check for
croc before we go bogi.

Nganjani

One time, when we got to the river we were not happy because a darrma had eaten the new jilgin net!

The Yard

Lots of our family work in the yard,
they cut the buliki tails and horns with clippers.
The buliki gets real mad and big fat
wet dribble from his mouth.

The Yard

Look at all the buliki.
One time in mustering season there were thousands of buliki in the yards …
and thousands of flies!
We saw a chopper coming.

The School

Here is our school.
Come inside and see all the fun things
we do with Miss Carolyn.

The School

Come outside and have a go on our big round swing.
We push you and spin you around and around real fast.
The dogs just watch.

Play basketball with us,
let's see who can get the ball in the hoop.

Yumob wandim plei at mi?
This is how you shudum goal!

The School

One time at school when we had biggest mob of rain, we ran out the classroom and danced in the rain. Some kids rode a shopping trolley through the flood!

The School

In the wet season, it rains and rains every day. Biggest mob of rain! Water covers the oval, airstrip and all the creeks are full.

Sometimes our Community is like an island.

KALANO
6Φ
CAM
2

Hunting

After school, we go hunting for bush turkey.
We drive for a long time, about half an hour.
Sometimes we see dingoes hanging around the buliki.
They run away when they see us come in the troopy.

One time, we got four bush turkey.
When we got back to camp, we pulled all their feathers out and shared them around.

One for blue house, one for white house, one for green house, and one for the old lady.

Everyone loves eating bush turkey and we had a good feed.
Next time you come too.

So many special places to go.
So many fun things to do.
This is where we play.
This is our home.
Amanbidji, Ngarinyman Country.

Glossary

There are two different First Languages in this book: Kriol and Ngarinyman. We have used colours to indicate which words belong to which language. The red words are Kriol and the green words are Ngarinyman.

The Kriol and Ngarinyman and traditional story in this book have been shared and edited with the guidance of the Community.

As first languages are traditionally oral, this text has been transcribed based on Community knowledge.

garu = kids

'Gedim my line, gwigbala one!' = 'Get my fishing line quick!'

'Wiii!!! Ei, Bronanna! Catfish and turtle. Luk darrei.' = 'Hey, Bronanna! Catfish and turtle. Look that way.'

bogi = swim

'He rait, wi wok brom iya!' = 'It's ok, we can walk from here!'

'Luk darrei. Jabiru!' = 'Look there. Jabiru!'

Nganjani = the Ngarinyman word for a place down by the river

dan.yan = bait fish

yawu = fish

girrawa = goanna

'Im hotwanbala!!!' = 'It's reeeeally hot!'

'Gu bogi!' = 'Let's swim!'

Lukad! = Careful!

darrma = crocodile

jilgin = yabbie

'Poor bala, no jilgin!' = 'Oh well, no yabbies!'

buliki = cow/cattle

'Ooo, ded bulagi tjigiwan!' = 'That cow is cheeky!'

'Yumob wandim plei at mi?' = 'You want to play with me?'

'This is how you shudum goal!' = 'This is how you shoot a goal!'

'Gaman, wi gu bogi!' = 'Come on, let's go swimming!'

'Dem dingo might be gedim buliki.' = 'The dingoes might get a cow.'

'It tastes good balawei!' = 'It tastes good way!'